invisible spaces

Invisible Spaces

Jack Alun

red hand
BOOKS

First published in 2022 by **Red Hand Books**
124, City Road, London
EC1V 2NX

www.redhandbooks.co.uk

Copyright©2022 by Jack Alun

ISBN 9781910346471

All rights reserved. No part of this edition may be used or reproduced in any manner whatsoever without the prior written permission of the copyright holder, except in the case of brief quotations embedded in critical articles or reviews.

A CIP catalogue record for this book is available from the British Library

Prepared for publication by Red Hand Books
Cover design © Red Hand Books

This book is sold subject to the condition that it shall not by way of trade or otherwise be lent, re-sold, hired out, or otherwise circulated without the publisher's prior consent in any form of binding or cover other than that which it is published and without a similar condition including this condition being imposed on the subsequent purchaser.

For Jill, Simon, Lucy, Lewis and Lauren, and for all the people who have made this project both viable and a success, especially Richard and Carole at Red Hand Books.

Acknowledgements

Versions of these poems have appeared in the following magazines: 'Mathematics' in *Poetry Wales*; 'Wavelengths' in *Spokes*; 'Circe' in *Argotist*; 'All at Sea' in *Coffee Shop*.

Apropos of nothing or maybe hoping to end a drought of ideas, I started rereading Homer's Odyssey. A strange time, as it happened – a lull before a storm, a phoney war – when nothing much, apart from two brief trips to Malta and Mallorca, seemed to be of stimulus. Then again, one can't quite ignore the connection between the two islands and their sea vistas and what I began to read. But, like everyone else, I couldn't imagine what was about to happen next.

I was in the process of formulating ideas for a series of poems around Odysseus's travels when Covid struck and the world, as we had experienced it, imploded, with all the curtailment and confinement that that implosion came to entail. Gradually, as the days mounted and with them a drift towards instrospection, my ideas began to take on a far more personal, inquiring approach in what I was writing, so that the result, *Invisible Spaces,* is a collection of poems that journeys both inwardly and outwardly, exploring encounters with a range of people, places and events through the mirage of a single mind, the invisible space.

Contents

Mathematics (Cosmeston Lakes, De Morgannwg)	3
Wavelengths (Tenby, Pembrokeshire)	4
The Dance (Cosmeston Lakes, De Morgannwg)	5
Tramp Beggar Actor King	6
Keep on dancing (Cardiff, De Morgannwg)	8
Evolution (Lunac, Aveyron)	10
Cities	11
A Lover's Farewell (to Calypso)	14
Circe (Thorney Island, West Sussex)	15
The Haunting (Plain of Venezia)	18
An Ice Cream (Rajasthan, India)	19
Heat (Delhi, India)	21
Lost (South East Asia)	23
Lessons from Nature (Southern India)	27
Alien (Madurai, Tamil Nadu)	30
All at sea (Berry Head, South Devon)	33
Going Under (Elberry Cove, Devon)	34
Underworld (Paris, France)	35
Three times dead	37
Inherit the Earth (Twisted Theology)	47

At times the mirror increases a thing's value, at times it denies it.
Italo Calvino
Invisible Cities, 1972

Mathematics (Cosmeston Lakes, De Morgannwg)

The white swan
Is an elegant two
Formed on the water's
Darkening page.

Now she glides, like one,
The perfect number,
Tinged with a redness
Of the sunken sun.

Then into evening shadow,
Like zero, she's gone,
The page ripples –
The signs all minus.

Wavelengths (Tenby, Pembrokeshire)

Black birds at the sea's edge
Bleak sun on a bend of beach
Wet-smooth or clumsy in the dunes
The sand skirrs in a tough wind

Her back to the Georgian town a nun
Shopping bag in hand busies by
Between dunes and tide to...

There is nothing beyond the sand and the rocks
And the grey clouds grinding and a headland
And the riding of a rolling sea on which Ireland
Surfs its wavelengths away

A shiver of sadness
At her single passing
Sisters the inward way
She flaps across the strand
This frail simple woman
Looking startled to be seen
Her rabbit eye scampering
The winter landscape for a home

Black birds at the sea's edge
Bleating like goats in a tough wind

The Dance (Cosmeston Lakes, De Morgannwg)

Light as a smile your mind
as you dance with a swan
on a wooden promontory
a day trip to the lake
sun splintering black water
white dots of gulls
the weave of ducks
the swan bends its neck
you your arms
twisting and parodying
in clumsy ease
neither here nor there
but somewhere
united in motion
to the clouds you've gone
wanton with grace
the swan
yourself
in twisting grimace –
until a stern voice summons
and with the bowing of your head
you rejoin the insanity of a world
your moment had fled.

Tramp Beggar Actor King

You bow to applause
the plaything of Fates
having passed the audition
the curtain awaits

The theatre has emptied
the script has been torn
the boom of your voice
a mere ghost that lives on

A weather flayed face
you shuffle the streets
sandals and no socks
on worn swollen feet

The scenery broken
the chorus profane
cast long disbanded
soliloquy reigns

****

tramp beggar
actor king
you live each part
of the play's the thing

no home but Thebes
or Elsinore
Dunsinane
or Prospero's shore

You've learnt the lines...
what more?

Keep on dancing (Cardiff, De Morgannwg)

time sweats
a shaven armpit
in an off-the-peg T

tall buildings
shadow a high life

days pass
texting of thrills

nights
without darkness

lyrics
that clamour

vibrations
in a chorus

repetition
can't stop

models of
e-dreams

electricity
in the beat
keep it neat

as the music
gets tighter...

and tighter

keep on dancing
why don't you

don't stop

Evolution (Lunac, Aveyron)

Once corruption
Was of a different kind
Air brushed and tinted
Dubbed as innocence
In ignorance of the past
So that now perplexed
When the global serpent
Entered the little village
With its mediaversal ways
Its 'knowing' and narcotics
Alluring fashion
And its shiny cars
That the ancient granite stone
Enticed became untrue
Or just true to itself
In a different way
Abandoning without regret
Its ancient oaks and rivers
Its language with the beat
And atavistic mystery
Of its untamed syllables
Its secrets and stories
And passed down wisdoms
Lingering just long
And faintly enough
On your eardrum
To detect in its dwindling
Until the little world came to speak
Like the big world glossy
With the colour of commerce.

Cities

When he thought of cities
He thought of Europe
He thought of Vienna and Rome
Paris and old Prague
Munich and Madrid
Barcelona and Brussels
Bordeaux and Budapest
Antwerp, Amsterdam
London and Lisbon
And Dublin and so on…

He thought of architecture
And culture and traditions
And tastes and smells
And vowel sounds
Their histories so tangible
He could slice chunks off them
With a mental knife
And lay them out
Segment by segment
For ingestion.

So was the goldfish bowl in which he swam
And the education that enmeshed him.

Cities which didn't immediately
Spring to mind
Like Los Angeles and Lima
Quito and Quebec
Bangkok and Burkina Faso

Mumbai and Melbourne
Canterbury and Cairo
Beijing, Buenos Aires
Johannesburg and Jerusalem
Were allowed to drift
Within those vague categories
Of a distant exclusion
(But not New York
Definitely not New York
New York was different)
Of the jumble of others
What did he know
That Los Angeles had Hollywood
Bangkok Buddhism
Beijing Tiananmen
Melbourne cricket
Burkina Faso a film festival
Buenos Aires the tango
And Jerusalem conflict
And the storybooks of
Crucifixions and crusades...
So in conclusion
And what remained
Were the lazy half-remembered
Sporadic fragments culled
To decorate the mask
Ornament his ignorance
A face on a face
Wisdom in a gaudy Max Factor
Pierrot to the slapstick of a clown.

A rhyme to perplexity:

If culture serves to make us blind
And travel emancipate the mind
What chance with home ingrained inside you
When an open mind is about to guide you

A Lover's Farewell (to Calypso)

Explorer of nights' infinities
an ageless photograph of time
enchantress of the seven circles
nebula of the divine
aglitter in sweat-soaked union
dark storms inside us raging
embracers of collusion
the world a distant ringtone
trite liturgy of illusion
that all truth requires
is mere desire
and desire the only truth –
slick tautology of confusion –
until daylight breaks on crusted eyes
and all good things must cease
and a road wind back
to a patient past
which lust cannot delay
you with yours and me with mine
heated centrally and indoors
where by her side I'll dream to share
the humdrum of tomorrow
so it's farewell now and always
let this necromance desist
so chains of lust unlink and rust
and a scribbling blind sea
sing of lone odyssey
through a spindrift of tales…
left untold.

Circe (Thorney Island, West Sussex)

Your taming charms
like prowling lions
made meat of me
turn men to beasts
and reason snout
in the piggeries
of human nature
the sweat of instinct
and contours of illusion

   ****

am I there with her

either with love

or with death

either the first taste

or the first touch

bonded between us

a soiled sheet

sacrament of intimacy

the intimate infinite

of opposites

or understanding

as the self she wore

the predisposed self

the self that never slept

with eyes wide open

and legs

only to be dreamed of

the cliché of images

flower in the garden

fruit in the orchard

champagne on the tongue

perfume of an empty room

lingering

lace on lingerie

skin against skin

the smoothness of eternity

of dark crescendo

executioner and executed

tumbling arms wrapped

through a baseless sky

to those somewheres

on the circumference of earth

where she resides

the forgetfulness

of a half-remembered song

now and then reprising

The Haunting (Plain of Venezia)

...while in the near-by distance
within shadowy reach
of a harvest of trees
earthy and ethereal
shimmering under the bushel
of the last day's warmth
a crumbling grain store
rib-roofed
and worm-worn
haunts with its secrets
in a spectral shade.

An Ice Cream (Rajasthan, India)

He should not
Have bought
That ice cream
In Jodhpur
With the extra
Buttermilk topping.
He knew it was
A risk at the time.
The Brahmin blue city
With its cubes of houses
The looming rectangle
Of fortress on the hill
Have faded from memory
Until all that remains
Is a busy little shop
In a grubby street
And the brief pleasure
Of a meltingly cold
Ice cream cone moment
Sticky
On his lips and fingers.
Not even the cries
Of the peacocks
From the Umaid Bhawan Palace
Reaching out to him
Through the night
And the years
Can refresh in his memory
Of the time or the space
Only the wail of his stomach

Clutched blindly beneath
The stabbing pain
Of a star-filled sky.

In Udaipur
He would only eat
Boiled eggs
For by then
His confidence had gone
So that when he saw
In the restaurant
The old blind sitar player
Being led from the room
By a prepubescent boy
It wasn't a welling of pity
He felt stirring inside
But something very different
And much
Much more intense.

Heat (Delhi, India)

Do you remember Delhi
Leaving the hotel in Connaught Place
In a summer which was so hot
That as soon as you got outside
You wanted to throw up on the pavement
And the plump Sikh taxi driver
Who misunderstood our destination
And drove us through the park pointing out
The seated courting couples
And later was miffed at not getting a tip
And the Baha'i temple so promising
White and shaped like a lotus flower
With its uniformed Korean custodians
Officious and briefed to keep visitors
From trampling the precise green grass
An impressive facade but with a hollow interior
A faith doomed to its good intentions
And the shush-shushing of its minders
And in a summer so sweltering and so dry
That people were dying in the streets
Hospitals crammed to their corridors
So they put you on an old stretcher
Where attached to a drip feed
In a corrugated iron shed
Used oxygen bottles
Dumped in a pile beside you
A western curio left
Abandoned to the life-saving
Monotony of a slow rehydration

Tell me –
Do you derive mood and picture
From the city's deconstruction
As it remains for us so long ago –
The sounds the tastes the smells the touch
The images and the images of images
Do they flit and focus like ghosts
Ariels full of mischief
Or do you flee them
As if pursued by a fiend?

Lost (South East Asia)

Do you remember
When you almost got lost
In the Himalayas
As you almost did once
In the Cameron Highlands
When if you'd turned right
Instead of left
You'd have buried yourself
Unmapped
In the denseness
Of forest there
Imprisoned by the trees
And if it hadn't been
For the neat pile
Of human defecation
In the undergrowth
Beside the path
That so revolted
And unnerved you
In the twilight
Of that lonely place
Causing you
To double back
Away from it
Then to your left
Which was right
Untangling you
Haltingly and blindly
From the dusk
Of that entombing forest

To the partial aperture
Then broadening light
Of a patterning sky?

You seldom took a map
Or a compass with you
Only an arrogant belief
In a sense of direction –
Lost to its own fallibility.

You'd never looked down
On the table of clouds before
Only from an aeroplane
Where mountain peaks
Protruded the tangibility
Of the rolling vapour
Then when a man
With a tied tight
Bundle of sticks
On the incline his back
Attached to a strap
Banded around his forehead
Passed without a word
And proceeded fleet foot
Down the winding path
Into the mountains
Which led to a nowhere
Of your imagining
And punctured the spell
Of your cloud filled reverie
Did you wake
To the turning
That you had to take

Directing you
Once again
To the left
Which was right
And on
Over an overgrown stile
Toward the searched-for solitude
And expectancy
Of a remote waterfall
Cool and shaded
In the repose
Of you imagining
Only for the reality
Of children's voices
Bouncing between boughs
And echoing through
The surrounding woodland
Where to be alone
At one with the sound of water
Adrift in altitudes of silence
Was by the fracture
Of those shrill
Childish voices
To be denied you
Because the conjured moment
Of your Zen was voiceless
And alone –
Whereas now
In the monotonies
Of the falling water
Only disappointment
At the tumble of its loss
Could ever remain.

The next day you caught
The narrow gauge
Toy train from Shimla
To Kalka where you sat
In a darkened waiting room
For the train to Delhi to arrive
The packed room was airless
And lazily rats sniffed
Round the silhouettes of luggage.

Lessons from Nature (Southern India)

From sands and rice pebbles
Of the multi-coloured beach
He gazed needy and gullible
But distinct as from
The minibus chatter
And tourists that surrounded him
In the concentration of his focus
Though not closely observed
Was an intensity a contraction
Within the constipation of that
Sacred moment
His mind intent
On squeezing meaning
However painful
From the brochured horizon
And limitless seascape
Of an unyielding subcontinent
A squinting statue
Beneath the frowning clouds
Of that salt smeared palette
Cape Comorin
The British had once called it
Fusing the illusion
And comfort of the familiar
With the arrogance of control.

So south
In Tamil Nadu
There where he is
Standing on the seashore

Near a small town
With a name of
The virgin goddess
Krishna's sister
Kanyakumari
Familiarly Shakti and Devi
The 'land's end' of India
Where the pearl rich
Laccadive sea
Meets the three waters
Of the Indian Ocean
The Arabian Sea
And Bay of Bengal
The one place on Earth
To watch the sunset
And sunrise from the ocean
Sacred in its simplicity
And where he was told
Ghandi's ashes
Had been scattered
But that was probably untrue.

Through the wave-
Washed moments
Duped and gullible
He too like the ashes
Of Ghandhi sought
From the three seas
To float, sacred and exemplary
Towards revelation

1. A bird flying with a fish in its beak is attacked mid-air by a bird of the same species. It wants to steal the fish that dangles tastily from the beak of the other, but in the fighting that follows the fish drops back into the sea. So, as neither bird gets to eat it, and must go to the trouble to fish or thieve for another, empty-beaked, they fly off.

2. Strong waves lap against the shore. Defiant, a small black crab clings to a grey rock. The weight and motion of the water seem always about to dislodge it – force against force – but it clings on. Stubborn in its purpose.

From the flexibility
Of signifiers
Before him
And naivety
Of purpose
He conjures
Two life lessons
From the narrative
Of Nature
And internalises.

Alien (Madurai, Tamil Nadu)

Who was the I
Who was the me

Back then
Or you?

What is to understand
Was that he would often
Confuse himself
With another
And was sad
That things were not so –
Just void.

On that long overnight
Train journey
To Madurai
Who was he looking for?

Later that day
He became deflated
Because the Temple
Of the town
Huge and grubby
And was overrun
By a franchised spirit
Of religious
Commercial chaos
Which didn't in any way
Fit (Not that

He was an expert
In such matters)
To be reminded only
How a place
Of worship should
Biblically be organised
By the fable
His childhood story
Of the driving out
Of the money lenders
From the commerce
Of that temple
In long ago Jerusalem
Which silently he too
Now dearly desired
Yet without confidence
The assuredness
And conviction
Of a Messiah
Could do nothing
But seethe
And inwardly churn.

So in search
Of the reassurance
Of peace
You sat alone
Beside the temple's
Bathing ghat
When a group
Of excited and chattering
Young boys
Came and sat

Around you
And 'Mr...'
One of them asked
'Mr... which country
You come from?'
'Mars,'
You replied easily
And without thinking.

All at sea (Berry Head, South Devon)

The bed deconstructs
on rocks of the storm
a back breaking pitch
in a lick sweat of rain
and thump humping of the wind

To a tide flow bite
salt as it's moist
wrestling the dominance of waves
in the dart and silver
provoke of the fish's art

Until the hollow gull echo
of a sob rent sky organs
to the crack and churn
of the white-water ride
in torment of breaker's writhing

Going Under (Elberry Cove, Devon)

A face
beneath the water
not my own
quizzes me
in layered ages
of itself
fear
as in a spinning stone
a castaway disc
of concentric selves
plunged inwards
as the wrinkled light
will widow faces
and the to fro
to fro
heave of the glass
blue water
draws shoals
of pattern
on the liquid life
of the blood sucking sea
above which wherever
whenever
the smug bulb
of an arcing sun
dangles brief
and flickers.

Underworld (Paris, France)

*"...but first there's another journey
you have to make," she said.*

July night
burning
once as now
heard engines
tick tock tick tock
slow down time
the circling of tyres
flow like water
on a sunken road
the moon cosying
to the buildings' cleavage
street-lamps (mantis
without prayer)
migrate
amid a calculus of hutches
their dim lights splaying
chorusing
without harmony
against the unseen
strumming of the stars
or high-heeled
to the perfumed
music of sirens
bodies to the night
adornments
in the shadow
of slave ships

profit and game
trapped between dispensable
and the one eyed
stony stare
to the marketing
and oblivion of pain
'...and you and I
let us drink
to addict and apostle the same
as to the unseen one
who loiters
in a vagrancy of doorways
a foul breathed wind
suffocating
like a remote memory
a presumptuous murmur
dealing hands
of small talk
to a purblind night.'

Three times dead

Driving after a weekend
Spent at Totleigh Barton Manor
Reputed once to have been
An old hunting lodge
Of King John's
And returning to Exeter
In my old black classic
Bullnose Morris 8
On which the sunroof
Had never slid back
And the driver's door
Which was hinged
Contra-logically
Towards the rear
And which tended
To open alarmingly
When negotiating
Sharp right-hand bends
Driving on tyres worn
Bald and shiny
As my grandpa's head
And the sun again shining
Though not brightly
After a long dry spell
And the mid-morning unremarkable
And chugging amiably by
When all of a sudden
An unforecast sharp shower
Bounced refreshingly
Off the windscreen

Of the car
Challenging the too small
Labouring wipers
And transforming the warm
Dry surface of the road
Into a skid track
Changing its relationship
With the car's
Four shiny tyres
From casual grip
To a smooth glide
With immediate effect
So when negotiating
The next not too sharp
Bend in the road
The car slipped sideways
And finding contact
With a grassy bank
Spun as if in slow motion
Rolled onto its side
And in a grind of metal
And tarmac
Slid across the road
My hand
Through the open window
Pressing against
The wet warm surface
Of the rough road
Expecting at any moment
To mangle or to lose it
Either that
Or it was having
My head

Bouncing
Like an overripe melon
About to split.

Facing the direction
From where I'd come
And on the opposite side
Of the road
The car reached
A grassy verge
And rolling twice
Crashed through a hedge
And landed upright
About ten yards
From a speechless farm worker
Bruised shocked
But certainly not speechless
I stood
My head and shoulders
Appearing
Through a surprisingly
Opened sunshine roof
And asked
Not for aid
Or forgiveness
But where
Dislodged from my foot
By the crash
Was my sandal
My only concern
As I stood there
A shocked idiot

A comic tank commander
In a buckle of metal.

The next early morning
The cash-in-hand mechanic
Who serviced my procession
Of clapped-out cars
Drove to the field
Where the inert black
Buckled wreck still stood
Towed the evidence
To another quiet field
Outside Exeter
And obligingly torched it
Should the police
Have decided
On a second
And closer look
At the smooth
And shiny black
Surfaces of the four tyres
Bald as my grandpa's head.

  ***

On Spinalonga
An island near the small
Tourist town of Elounda
Fortified by the Venetians
Who gave it its name
Meaning 'long thorn'
And once used as a refuge

By besieged Ottomans
Sheltering from the wrath
Of angry Christians
And latterly the twentieth century
As a leper colony.

Crossing from the Cretan
Mainland with a group
Of rowdy holiday friends
We entered the fortification
Through the Dante's Gate
The way the lepers would have done
Noisy flip-flopping tourist lepers
Hung over from the night before
Retsina, ouzo, beer
Moussaka followed by
Some rugged grilled meat and chips
And like stumbling
Sunken-eyed zombies
Swarmed out among the ruins
Bouncing voices off the cold
Inarticulate inertness
Of the old stones as if
Frightened by their silence
And to endow them once again
With imagined life
Some having their photographs
Taken lying in empty graves
Others posing in doorways
Or clambering high
On the surviving walls
My head still throbbing
From the previous evening

And feeling unsociable
I wandered off
To explore the curious
Dusty little island
My bulky SLR Nikon
Weighty around my neck
The sea beating in the wind
On the rocks below
The ancient fortification walls
A strong wind as is often
In those parts dry
And alarmingly thirst inducing
I climbed circumspectly
Onto the dizzying rampart
For the drama of a steeper angle
Before shuffling along the dusty top
My eye to the lens…
I don't know what stopped me
But another pace
And I'd have been over the edge
Splayed and broken on the rocks below
Careless through my hangover
I'd attached a 35mm
Wide angle lens to the camera
Instead of the usual 50
So that the optics of that distortion
Bending my eye came very close
To the reality of the far from picturesque
Freefall of my annihilation
Heart pounding and hands shaking
I rejoined the hilarity of my new friends
And forcing the broadest of smiles
Said nothing.

***

This is perhaps the feeblest
Of the might have beens
But no way less haunting
Impetuous and indicative
Of a flaw in character
On the Greek island
Of Kos in the Dodecanese
And nearing the summit
Of a dusty track
It was a hot day
And my legs ached as I climbed
When it started me thinking
That this'd be great
For labouring up
On a hired moped
Reaching the top
Then powering down
The as yet unseen slope
On the other side
Which I already sensed
In the pit of my stomach
And sure enough
Approaching the top
I could make out
The smoothly inviting crest
Which my mind
Was already accelerating over
Only over was out
Down and out
A flying descent

On to the rocks
And translucent blue below
Because the actual path
Turned abruptly left
That instead of achingly
Sweatingly walking
As I was now doing
I'd recklessly driven
My imaginary hired moped
Tearing blindly over the crest
I'd have died
Flying through the air
Clinging desperately
To the handlebars
Of an accelerating machine
This may have never happened
Only it did happen and does
Each time the picture leaks
And my stomach embarks
Again on its long descent
Neither drowning nor broken
But suspended always
Between cliff edge
And ever accusing
Translucence of the sea below.

    ***

But who knows
Maybe it's the final death
The expected one
That'll be most surprising
The realisation that not only

Has your luck run out
Time too
But that your body
Is crumbling slowly
Painfully piece by piece
Until you are no longer
Who you were
Though dagger sharp
Your mind may
Otherwise protest
Hoping hungering
For the impossible possible
That once was so easy
Taken for granted
Airy and light
Skipped by unnoticed
Not the ache of ageing
The torment and the torture
Like an endless scalding
Or like my favourite aunt
Weeping one day
At the cruel awareness
That creeping dementia
Would never go away.

Afterthought

Inherit the Earth (Twisted Theology)

God said to Adam
'I'll give you the earth
Just one condition
You don't know what it's worth
Innocent you might be
Wise you are not
Seeker after pleasure
Of outcomes not hot
I'll give you the forests
The land and the sky
The air that you breathe in
The seasons that go by
I'll give you the mountains
The lakes and the sea
Gratitude's one things
Respect's due to me'

'Too much', said Adam,
With a smile and a simper
'Can I do what I like there
Can I do it in temper
Can I do it in mischief
Can I do it like a thief
Can I do it for my children
The future human race
Can we dig in the earth
For fuel for machines
That we'll build to exude
Create great ravines
To hell with the dirt

To hell with the smog
The fucked over ozone
And the tree's final log
So what do you think dad
Am I'm qualified for that
To inherit the earth
Created on a whim
Never knowing its worth.'

'That's my boy,' said God
With a serious frown
'You're the one for me
When the chips tumble down
The one I can trust
So here for support
And total diversion
I'll throw in my gift
A wealth of quotation
The one Holy Bible
Which all peoples can trust
Believe me my boy
When the rivers run dry
And the world turns to dust
Serpent and Grim Reaper
You were as their keeper
Now let's embellish the job
You
As a stand-in benevolent God.'

Lightning Source UK Ltd.
Milton Keynes UK
UKHW021009180123
415553UK00015B/1093